MEALS A LA TICA
Costa Rican Cookbook

by Sandy

641.59
S222m Sandy, seud.
          Meals a la tica: Costa Rican cook book / Sandy
          – 4a. ed. – San José, C. R.: O. Sandí P., 2005.
          108 p.; 21 x 14 cm.

          ISBN 9968-9456-1-7

          1. Cocina costarricense. 2. Recetario. I. Título.

Original title: *Comidas a la tica.* © Orlando Sandí Peña (Sandy), 2004.

Translated by:
Óscar Aguilar Sandí
ninobueno@starmedia.com
angeldemonio@costarricense.cr

Typing and Graphic Design:
Jeannette E. Alvarado Achío
jalvarado1@costarricense.cr

Cover Design and Internal Illustrations:
Guillermo Ponce Alvarado

Sandy's email: **sandyescrit@hotmail.com**

"MEALS A LA TICA
Costa Rican Cookbook"

Sandy

CONTENTS

Page

DEDICATION

To great Vichi:
Thank you your fine meals: the chayote pi-
cadillo, the tortillas and the supreme main
course for a Tico yokel: the "olla de car-
ne".

Your recipes have not been revealed, the
post is still vacant…¡There is not any cook!

Sandy

ACKNOWLEDGEMENTS

To Mother Earth, to our country men, farmers and cooks who together, supply us with the food for our subsistence.

Affectionately for my people and, above all, those with a sweet-tooth!

Sandy

Sandy

PRESENTATION

When we touch the topic of Costa Rican cuisine, we have entered the heart of our very culture. With love, we prepare the recipes of the various dishes that are a part of our cultural stock and the idiosyncrasy of the Costa Rican people.

This cookbook is a culinary contribution, but at the same time it constitutes an invaluable attachment for your small laboratory, where the pots and cauldrons are your test tubes. In them, we will discover why to consume our own, getting away from the imported meals that purport to relegate our beloved habits.

Another wide range of dishes from the Central Valley obtains, and we hope to compile them next; not the commercial shape they are made in but the most traditional one. Among them, the rice cake figures, formerly known as the "torta de novios" ("Newly weds' cake"). It used to be the favorite food at weddings. From there this saying sprang: "Se jaló torta" ("She pulled a cake towards herself"), applied when a maid surrendered herself before getting married. (That is, she had eaten her newly weds' up without having a wedding, as it was the rule). Besides it that, there are the *piononos*, the *enlustrados*, the *quesadillas*, the *polvorones*, the *prestiños*, the *manjarete*, the *chinchiví* or ginger beer, the *cocadas*, the *bozas* or coconut candies, the *zapotillos*, the preserved chiverre, the grapefruit jelly and the guava jelly. All of them, unsurpassed delicacies.

On using them we express our people's friendly character. New generations of my country and citizens around the world: I invite you to taste the diverse dishes you will find inside these pages.

Sandy

SCIENTIFIC NAMES
OF SOME VEGETABLES

Achiote: Bixa orellana

Aki (Seso vegetal): Blighia sapida

Arracache: Arracacia xantorrhiza

Ayote: Cucurbita maxima

Burío: Apeita tiborbuo

Calalú: Amaranthus gagenticus

Chayote: Sechium edule

Chicasquil orquelite: Jathropha aconifolia

Chile panameño: Capsicum Sp.

Chiverre: Cucurbita Sp.

Camote: Ipomea batata

Fruta de pan (Breadfruit): Atocarpus sommuris

Itabo: Yuca elephantiples

Ñame: Dioscoreaceae tripida

Ñampí: Dioscoreaceae trifida

Piñuela: Ananas Sp.

Pipián: Cucurbita Sp.

Susumba: Solanum mammosun

Tacaco: Cucurbita Sp.

Tiquisque: Canthosoma ciolaceum

Vainica: Phaseolus vulgaris

Yuca: Manihot esculenta

Zapallo: Cucurbita moschata

TYPICAL MEALS FROM THE CENTRAL VALLEY
(San José, Alajuela, Heredia, Cartago)

Sandy

RICE PUDDING

Ingredients:

1/2 kg of rice
3 bottles of milk
2 cupfuls of sugar
1 yolk
1 little spoonful of cornstarch
   Some cinnamon chips or lemon rind

Preparation:

Boil the rice along with the cinnamon or the rind. Simmer it until it's ready and dried up. Reserve a cup of milk. Add the remainder of the milk and the sugar to the rice. Simmer it so that the rice acquires the flavor of the milk.

It must turn out being watery, so stir it constantly so that it doesn't stick. When almost ready, dissolve the cornstarch and the yolk in the cupful of milk you left aside. Now, add it to the rice, stirring strongly.

ARROZ CON POLLO

Ingredients:

4   cupfuls of rice
3 or 4 chopped-up breasts
1   medium-sized onion
2   bell peppers
2   finely minced celery branches
1   kg tomatoes or two spoonfuls of tomato paste
1/2 kg of carrots
      Garlics, pepper, cumin, Worcestershire sauce to taste.
      If wished, some raisins, olives and peas are added too.

Preparation:

Mince an onion and 1 bell pepper and put them into a pot along with some oil or fat. Add the breasts which were marinated with some salt, cumin, garlic and pepper. Once the breasts are a little brown, add the peeled and minced tomatoes or the tomato paste, besides enough water to cover them. Once softened, take them from the heat, let them cool a bit, and chop them up into pieces in a regular size.
As for the broth, strain it and add more water up to complete the amount for cooking the rice together with the vegetables and the spices.
When ready, add the chopped up chicken.

PIECES OF BOILED LOIN

Ingredients:

1   kg of loin, tenderloin or sirloin
     Some salt, garlic, pepper
1   pack of tomato soup
     Some fat to fry

Preparation:

Split the loin into not too big chunks, marinate it and fry it lightly
in the hot fat. Mix the tomato soup in with the juice given off the
loin. You can also cook some string beans and carrots to
accompany the loin.

CHAYOTE CHANCLETAS
Just good!

Ingredients:

3   ripe chayotes
1   bar of butter
1/4 kg of grated cheese or mincemeat
     Sugar to taste

Preparation:

Cut the chayotes in half and put them to boil with a pinch of salt. When ready, remove them from the heat and take their whole pulp out with a spoon. Discard the internal fiber known as "chuspa", but keep the entire peel bowls.
Prepare the pulp in the shape of a puree mixed with cheese, mincemeat or poultry. Stuff the peel bowls with the puree and bake them.

CHORREADAS

Ingredients:

12   unripe corncobs
1/2   an unit ("*tapa*") of unrefined sugar
1/4   kg of vegetal fat

Implements:

A corn grinder
A knife
A basin
A *comal* (kind of skillet)

Preparation:

Take the corn husks away and clean the cobs thoroughly. Scrape them with the knife and grind the grains. Catch the juice given off the grains and store it in the basin. Scrape finely the brown sugar and mix it with the ground corn. Pour some corn juice on it and make an even mixture.
Heat the comal. Put a little spoonful of fat and three spoonfuls of the paste in. When the chorreada is brown on one side, turn it round for browning the other one.
Serve them hot and topped by some sour cream or cheese.
Acompany them with a smashing good *agua dulce* (unrefined sugar dissolved in hot water).

CHIVERRE EMPANADAS

Chiverre:

Buy a chiverre that sounds when shaken (a sign of not being too ripe, in which case it would be full up of liquid). But be careful to choice a bruiseless one. Bake it at 350° F for an hour approximately. Then take it out and let it cool. When cool, split it to remove the seeds and a thin vein from the middle, as it would make the chiverre bitter. Mash it for it to be easier to tear. Drain it over a cheesecloth strainer or a cloth, and make the stuffing on the next day.

An alternative way to prepare the chiverre is as follows: purchase one with sound, and smash it against the floor in order that the pulp comes off more easily. Make use of a knife for that. Take all the seeds out and place the chiverre in some boiling water to soften it. Tear it into strands and wash it well. Drain it in a strainer. Then cook it along with 1 or 2 units of unrefined sugar, some cinnamon chips, the juice of one lemon and some grated lemon rind. Cook it until drying it up. You will love this variant.

Molasses:

1 or 2 units of unrefined sugar (depending on the size of the chiverre and how sweet you like it), some cloves, some cinnamon chips, 1 or 2 fig leaves.

Stuffing for the empanadas:

Cook the ingredients of the molasses but prevent it to thicken too much. Immerse the torn chiverre and let it dry a little up.

Dough for the empanadas:

2   bars of butter
220 g of cheese spread
3   cupfuls of flour
      A pinch of salt
      A pinch of sugar
      Some melted ice

Mix the dry ingredients with the margarine until they get crumbly. Add the cheese and water needed to make the dough manageable. Put it inside a plastic bag and refrigerate for two hours at least. Spread it with a rolling pin. Cut it in circles; stuff them with the chiverre jelly you prepared, join their edges and close them rightly by crushing with a fork. Paint every empanada with a mixture of yolks and milk, then sprinkle them with sugar and bake them on a greased tray.

CHEESE EMPANADAS

Ingredients:

2   bars of butter
2   cupfuls of flour
2   spoonfuls of sugar
2   cupfuls of grated cheese
1   whisked egg
1/2 a little spoonful of salt

Implements:

A rolling pin. A cook brush. An oven

Preparation:

Using your hands, mix the margarine, the flour, the sugar and the salt to make some soft dough which doesn't stick to your fingers. If some more flour is needed, add it little by little. Then flour a table. There, spread the dough by the rolling pin or a floured bottle. Cut the dough into some little circles using the lip of a glass or cup. Place a bit of cheese in the center of each circle and now fold it to shape an empanada. With the cook brush, apply little strokes of whisked egg all on the edges of the empanadas. Close them by pressing with the prongs of a fork. Put them on an ungreased tray. Bake them at medium heat for 15 minutes, or until they brown. Serve them hot.

ENYUCADOS

Ingredients:

2   kg of yucca
1   melted bar of margarine
115 g of non-fat (Turrialba) cheese
4   yolks
1   small onion
1   bell pepper
    Salt and pepper to taste
2   cloves of garlic
    Some flour
2   whisked eggs
    Some breadcrumb

Preparation:

Once washed and peeled, boil the yucca in salted water. Mince very finely the onion, pepper and garlic, and grate the cheese. Mix them in and add the butter. Continue to mix. Make some balls and stuff them with meat or even more cheese. Fold them into flour, egg and breadcrumb. Immerse it in pretty hot oil. At last, dry them off the oil over paper towels.

Meat stuffing:

250 g of mincemeat
1   finely minced small onion
1/2 finely minced bell pepper
1   spoonful of Worcestershire sauce
2   spoonfuls of oil

1   little spoonful of achiote
      Some salt and pepper
1   whisked egg

Fry lightly the onion and the bell pepper at low heat. Add the Worcestershire sauce, salt and pepper. Place the mincemeat in the frying pan and cook it until it changes its color. Process the mincemeat with the mixed spices to compact them fairly. Add the egg. Then remove the stuffing from the heat. Let it cool.

Cheese stuffing:

100 g of grated non-fat (Turrialba) cheese
1   finely minced small onion
100 g of grated cheddar
1   ounce of butter

Fry lightly the onion in the butter. Let it cool down. Mix it with both cheeses.

SQUASH CUSTARD

Ingredients:

2   cupfuls of a diced ripe squash ("*ayote*", *Cucurbita spp.*)
4   cupfuls of milk
4   little spoonfuls of cornstarch
    Some cinnamon, vanilla and sugar to taste

Preparation:

Boil the squash in rather little water. When soft, mash it in the same water until pureeing it. Add 3 cupfuls of milk, the cinnamon and the vanilla. Aside, dissolve the sugar and the cornstarch in the remaining cupful of milk. Add it to the puree, stirring constantly to keep it from sticking. Let it dry to taste, and serve it cold.

ORANGE CUSTARD

Ingredients:

3   cupfuls of water for cooking the rice
3/4 a cupful of sugar
1/2 a cupful of raw rice
     The rind of an entire orange
1   can of condensed milk
1/2 a can of orange juice
4   eggs
1/2 a cupful of crystallized fruit

Implements:

A custard mold and a blender

Preparation:

Make a caramel by melting the sugar at low heat and pour it on the custard mold, impregnating it round inside. In the other hand, boil the rice along with the orange rind until the water evaporates. Then discard the rind and blend the rice with the condensed milk, the juice and the eggs for three minutes. Take it from the blender. Finally, add the crystallized fruit and mix them in fairly.

CHICKPEAS WITH PORK RIBS

Ingredients:

1/2   kg of chickpeas
1/2   kg of pork ribs
2   sliced green plantains
2   diced tomatoes
2   bell peppers
2   minced onions
1/2   a spoonful of sugar
       Some oil, garlic, oregano, coriander, achiote

Preparation:

The day before, wash the chickpeas and put them to soak. Afterwards, boil them in enough water with a little salt. Remove them from heat when they start to soften. Wash the pork ribs and cut them into pieces. Boil them together with some salt, onion, garlic, oregano and coriander. Fry the diced tomatoes in oil and achiote.

Add to these the sugar, the onion, some salt, the sliced plantains and the chopped peppers. Put a lid on them and let them boil for some 15 minutes.

Finally, add the chickpeas, their broth, the pork and its bouillon. Boil everything for half an hour more.

OLLA DE CARNE
The feast dish for the Tico yokels

Ingredients:

1   kg of beef bones
2   liters of water
2   cloves of garlic
1   bell pepper
1   little bunch of coriander
1   leaf of celery
1   medium onion
1   big tomato (for some sauce)
1   branch of thyme
2   green plantains
2   corncobs
2   unripe chayotes
6   tacacos
1   big carrot
1/2   kg of potatoes
1/2   kg of squash
1/4   kg of tiquisque
1/4   kg of ñampí
1   medium sweet potato
1   pinch of achiote
      Salt to taste

Implements:

A big iron pot or pressure cooker

Preparation:

Boil the meat during 45 minutes together with the garlic, coriander, celery, bell pepper, onion, thyme and tomato.

Afterwards, add these vegetables that delay most to get cooked, that's green plantains, corncobs, chayotes, tacacos and tiquisques. Boil them for about 20 minutes.

At last, put inside the pot: the potatoes and sweet potatoes, the yucca, the squash, the carrot, the ñampí, the pinch of achiote and the salt.

You can serve the vegetables and the beef in a dish aside from the bouillon, or serve it all together as well.

ARRACACHE PICADILLO

Ingredients:

1 1/2 kg of arracache
1/2   kg of seasoned mincemeat
1/2   kg of sausage salami
4   well crushed cloves of garlic
1   finely minced bell pepper
1   finely minced bunch of coriander
1   pinch of achiote
4   chicken stock cubes or 1 cupful of concentrated
      chicken stock
3   peeled and split big tomatoes
2   spoonfuls of oil
      Pepper and salt to taste

Implement:

A grinder

Preparation:

Peel the raw arracache while you keep it under water. Mince it pretty finely and grind it too.
Wash it well and boil it softly some twice; then, let it drain.
In a pot, heat the oil and add the garlic, bell pepper, onion, coriander and achiote. Fry them lightly. Then, add the tomatoes, the mincemeat and the salami, and cook all until to get a good sauce.
Put in there the pepper and salt besides the chicken stock. Now, add the arracache and cook it at medium heat, until the picadillo feels soft. It must nevertheless turn out as dry as possible.

CHAYOTE PICADILLO

Ingredients:

3   chayotes
2   cloves of garlic
     Salt to taste
1   little spoonful of sugar
     Some achiote and fat

Implements:

A pot

Preparation:

Peel the chayotes and take the sap off them by immersing in water for five minutes. Mince them finely.
Fry the garlic (finely minced too) with some fat and salt.
It gives for 5 people. Serve it into *gallos* (wrapped in tortillas).

GREEN PLANTAIN PICADILLO

Ingredients:

2   green plantains
1/4 kg of sausage salami
1   minced big onion
1   cupful of milk
2   little spoonfuls of pepper
2   eggs
     Salt to taste
1   big tomato
1   minced big bell pepper
2   spoonfuls of oil

Preparation:

Boil the green plantains, peel them and mash them rightly. Put the oil in a frying pan, fry the onion and the bell pepper.
Add the sausage salami and stir all of them until right fried. Now add the tomato, the mashed plantain, the pepper and the salt. Whip the eggs, add them to the milk and pour on the plantain picadillo.

OLD HEN SOUP
It revives even the dead!

Ingredients:

1	old home hen, duly plucked and cleaned
2	liters of water
1/4	kg of yucca
1/2	kg of potatoes
1	kg of potatoes
1	unripe chayote
1	small carrot
1	bell pepper
1	small onion
2	cloves of garlic
1	little bunch of coriander
1	leaf of celery
1	little branch of thyme
1	pack of "angel hair" noodles
1	pinch of achiote
	Salt to taste

Implements:

Either 1 large pot or a pressure cooker

Preparation:

Boil the chicken for an hour or more, depending on how soft it turns. Add the bell pepper, the onion, the coriander, thyme and garlic. Straightaway, split every vegetable into small pieces and join them all in the pot.
The time of cooking is 25-35 minutes, and the recipe gives for 6 people.

BLACK SOUP
A remedy for the mellow tipplers' hangovers

Ingredients:

1/2	kg of black beans
1	liter of water
1	little branch of oregano
1	big onion
2	cloves of garlic
1	little branch of thyme
4	eggs
	Salt to taste
1	small bunch of coriander

Implements:

A medium pot or a pressure cooker
A strainer
A blender

Preparation:

Put the beans to boil along with the garlic, the oregano and the thyme. Remain on it until the beans soften.

Then strain them. Take two cupfuls of bean broth to the blender and add a cupful of beans. Once blended, pour the broth on a small pot and heat it up. Add the coriander, the onion and the four eggs one by one, slowly. The cooking lasts 5 minutes.

TAMAL ASADO

Ingredients:

1/2 kg of corn paste
1/4 kg of white cheese
1   egg
1/2 a bottle of fresh or sour milk
1/8 kg of sugar
1   pinch of salt
1/4 kg of margarine
1   cupful of grated coconut

Preparation:

Grate the cheese. Slowly, add the milk to the corn paste, beating with your hands to dissolve pellets. Then, add the cheese, the melted margarine, the salt, the coconut and the sugar. Mix everything well. Grease a saucepan, pour the mix on it, and bake. When brown, let it cool and cut it in squares.
The proof to know when it is already baked is inserting a knife. Does it come out dry? It's ready.

PORK TAMALES

Ingredients:

1	kg of pork ribs
2	liters of water
2	bunches of coriander
2	bell peppers
1	whole garlic
1	leaf of oregano
1	leaf of thyme
1	little package of cumin powder
2	kg of corn paste
1	kg of potatoes
1/2	kg of string beans
1/2	kg of carrots
1/2	kg of peas
1	kg of rice
1	pinch of achiote
2	kg of plantain leaves for wrapping the tamales
1	roll of wick tie

Implements:

A corn grinder
A knife
A mincing board
A large pot
A basin
A strainer

36

Preparation:

Boil the pork along with all the ingredients for 45 minutes. Boil the potatoes, grind them and mix them with the paste and the pork stock.

Stuffing for the tamale:

Tear the plantain leaves in segments. Take two spoonfuis of the paste and add 1 spoonful of rice, some strips of bell pepper, some pieces of carrot, string beans, peas and a chunk of pork. Then wrap it in the plantain leaves and tie it with the wick. The time of cooking is 45 minutes within a boiler.

CORNSTARCH TAMAL

Ingredients:

500 g of cornstarch
500 g of sugar
250 g of grated cheese
250 g of butter
3   cupfuls of fresh milk
3   cupfuls of sour milk
3   cupfuls of water
1   spoonful of salt

Implements:

A wooden spoon. An oven a mold. A knife.

Preparation:

Blend both kinds of milk with the water in a pot. Add the sugar,
the cornstarch, the cheese, the butter and the salt. Simmer it,
stirring constantly with the wooden spoon until it bubbles. Pour
the mix in a greased casserole or mold and take it to the oven.
Let the tamal get a thin coat that is a bit dark, but it does not
have to brown wholly.
On cooling down, it hardens. Once cool, you may cut it in
squares.

CRYSTALLIZED GRAPEFRUIT

Ingredients:

1	big grapefruit, rather green
4	cupfuls of water
1/2	a little spoonful of bicarbonate
1	pound of sugar
10	cloves
10	drops of coloring (beet or carrot juice may be used instead)
2	fig leaves, if wished.

Preparation:

Peel the grapefruit and divide it into segments of some 3 cm in width. Take the inner part away and keep the thick white shell. Leave them in water over 24 hours (a whole day), changing the water at several times. Passed this time, drain the segments well and boil them in some water and bicarbonate; let it just bubble. Then, shift them to a board for draining again. Once cool, end the draining by crushing every segment with your hand.

Into a pot, mix the 4 cupfuls of water with the sugar, the cloves and the coloring. Take them to boil. Then add the segments of grapefruit and cover them with the fig leaves. Remain cooking it for some three hours, waiting for it crystallizes. If you notice whitish, non-crystallized areas, prick them with the prongs of a fork so that the syrup goes in.
If you wish, after the grapefruit has cooled, sprinkle it with sugar.

ITABO FLOWER OMELETTE
None remain without taste it!

Ingredients:

1   itabo flower bunch
1   onion
2   tomatoes
4   spoonfuls of butter or margarine
2   hard-boiled eggs, finely minced
     Some breadcrumb
     Some grated cheese

Preparation:

Remove the central parts from the flowers as they would give a bitter taste off the dish. Boil the itabo in salted water for some minutes, and then, drain it.

Apart, on a frying pan, fry the minced onion and the tomatoes in the butter. Add some salt and pepper and the itabo as well. If you feel like it, add the minced eggs, the cheese powder and the breadcrumb. Serve it hot.

Alternatively, you can bake it for some minutes on a greased casserole, with more cheese powder and breadcrumb over the top.

CORN AND CHEESE TORTILLAS

Ingredients:

1   kg of corn paste
1/2 kg of grated cheese
6   glassfuls of water
     Salt to taste

Implements:

1 basin
1 comal
1 broiler

Preparation:

Put the corn paste, the cheese, the salt and the water in the basin, and knead them.

Then, slap the paste to give it the shape of tortillas. Cook them on the heated-up comal for one minute. After cooking the first side, turn it over for a more minute. Shift the tortillas to the broiler for even a more minute.

Now, they are ready for you to help to them, with some sour cream on top and drinking a glassful of the superb Costa Rican coffee.

The recipe gives for 25 medium-sized tortillas.

STUFFED ZUCCHINIS

Ingredients:

8   unripe *zapallitos* or zucchinis
250   g of mincemeat
1   minced onion
2   spoonfuls of fat
4   spoonfuls of breadcrumb
2   spoonfuls of cheese powder
2   eggs
      Salt, garlic, oregano and pepper to taste

Implements:

A frying pan, a little spoon and maybe, an oven

Preparation:

Boil the zucchinis in salted water. Once softened, drain them.
Put the fat on a frying pan and fry just lightly the onion and the
garlic. Add the mincemeat. Let it get cooked for some minutes.
Add the oregano, the pepper, the cheese powder, the
breadcrumb and the eggs. Mix them well and let them cool
down.
Cut a little slice out of one of the tips of each zucchini, and
making use of a little spoon, take the pulp and the seeds off.
Stuff them with mincemeat. Place them on a greased tray and
bake them. Don't you have an oven close at hand? Don't worry.
Make a tomato sauce and boil the zapallitos in for some minutes.
You can also fold them into some breadcrumb and a whisked
egg, and then fry them. Anyway, they are scrumptious!

TYPICAL MEALS
OF GUANACASTE
(North Pacific)

SANDY

ARROZ DE MAÍZ

Ingredients:

1	big chicken
1	kg of white or yellow corn
1	big tomato
4	whole garlics
1	spoonful of pepper and cumin seed
5	leaves of "coyote" (native) coriander
250	g of carrots
250	g of vegetal fat
1	big onion
2	spoonfuls of lard
	Salt and achiote to taste

Implements:

A strictly wooden spoon

Preparation:

Boil the chicken in three bottles of water with garlic and salt, until softening it right. Keep it apart. Meanwhile, after having soaked and washed the raw corn, break it so that it turns into fine grain, something like rice. Wash it to remove the corn trash and keep that water, just filter it out.

Now, boil the broken corn in the chicken bouillon. Add the seasonings one by one, and the lard too. Finally, add the chicken, once you have it well *"despenicado"* (cut up).

Simmer it, taking care of not smoking it. As the bouillon seeps, add the water that remained from boiling the corn. The arroz de maíz must turn out soft and watery, so take advantage of that corn water.

45

ARROZ GUACHO

Ingredients:

1	kg of pork ribs
750	g of rice
1/2	a spoonful of pepper
1	big onion
2	spoonfuls of vinegar
4	cloves of garlic
4	leaves of native coriander
2	small bell peppers
1/2	little spoonfuls of achiote
3	leaves of oregano
3	spoonfuls of lard
1	little sprout of peppermint
	Salt to taste

Implements:

An iron cauldron

Preparation:

At first, marinate the pork. Afterwards mince it. Put it in the cauldron to boil with the other ingredients. Softened the meat, add the raw rice (after washing and draining it). Mix everything and cover the contents of the cauldron with boiling water. Softened the rice (not cooked), stir it to equalize the cooking degree. Add enough water to cover the pork, and put the lid on to prevent it from drying up. By this it's called "arroz *guacho*" (it means "soft and thin").

ATOL PUJAGUA

Ingredients:

1   a liter of purple corn
8   units of unrefined sugar

Implements:

A cheesecloth strainer
A wooden spoon
The tradition is to use an earthenware pot or *nimbuera*

Preparation:

Soak the purple corn. After 8 hours, break it and grind it finely. Still raw, dissolve it in water until it gets "*atolón*" (somewhat watery). Strain it. Purify it by running water for discarding the *payana* or rubbish.

This atol remains untouched until the next day, when it has got some bitterness and the paste is settled. With a clean pot, decant a little of this pink water off and keep it aside. It will give the desire consistency to your atol. Put the atol to cook together with the scraped unrefined sugar and stir it continuously with the wooden spoon, to keep it from smoking or sticking. When it turns too thick, thin it by some pink water.

As long as you are cooking, taste the sweetness to make sure it doesn't go short because the added pink water. It's accustomed to add a pinch of salt to the scraped unrefined sugar, to get the best taste.

Once cooked and thickened as wished, move it from heat and pour on small bowls or soup dishes, to let it cool down. It is really delicious still hot, but cool it is too, and even more one-day old.

Many people eat it adding some spoonfuls of milk and cream which make it gorgeous.

STEAMED MEAT

Ingredients:

2 1/2 kg of salted dry meat
6   ripe plantains
3   green plantains
      Enough salt

Implements:

Some lightly toasted plantain leaves
Some little wooden sticks from orange tree, *jícaro* tree or another
one that does not give any flavor off
1 large iron or clay pot

Preparation:

Salt the meat up, or instead, leave it for two days in the sun
under a net, to avoid flies. The day to fix it, take the large pot
and put at bottom a bed of small wooden sticks that are crossed.
However, leave an accurate distance of four inches from the
bottom to the bed, as the idea is the water doesn't cover the
sticks.
Over the bed of sticks lay a coat of plantain leaves. Over these,
put a layer of peeled plantains (so much ripe and green). Over
them, put a layer of meat. Then put another layer of plantains
and so on until the ingredients run out.
On the top of the uppermost layer, lay some more leaves and
set the lid. On boiling the water at bottom, it turns into steam
that is unable to go out. So it will coddle the meat and the
plantains. The steaming process takes four hours at least,
according to the amount of meat. Take care to renew the little
water by adding some more boiling water, but never overrun
the stick bed. You realize when the water has seeped by means
of the sound.

PIPIÁN DESSERT

Ingredients:

1   ripe pipián of 1/2 a kilo in weight
1   unit of unrefined sugar or, if preferred, 1 1/2 kg. of refined
     sugar
     Cloves to taste

Preparation:

Peel the pipián. Split it in large slices (of 1 or 2 inches). Take
some innards off the slices and boil them for roundabout ten
minutes. Then take them out and drain them.
Make the sugar into molasses with a little water, and cook it at
high heat along with the cloves. When the molasses is bubbling,
add the slices of pipián and lower the heat. Let it get coddled.
Once ready, remove from the heat. Serve it as a dessert, it's
unforgettable.

AJIACO

Ingredients:

500 g of pork ribs
500 g of bacon, not too greasy
3   sliced ripe plantains
2   sliced unripe corncobs
250 g of rice or otherwise white corn
1   dozen of chicasquil or quelite leaves
125 g of pork skin
500 g of peeled ripe squash in small pieces
1   small unit of unrefined, scraped sugar

Implements:

A mincing board. An earthen or iron pot

Preparation:

The day before, marinate the pork with some salt, pepper, achiote and garlic. Salt the bacon. The day to fix it, boil the bacon and the pork together with the plantain, the squash, the corncobs and the spices. On feeling the meat soft, take it out from the pot and dice it on the board. Put the diced meat in the pot again, and add the rice or the corn, whatever preferred. The corn has had to be ground roughly, so that the grains seem rice. Add the pork skin too.
Quickly boil the chicasquir or quelite in some salted water, just to soften the leaves. Take them out, mince them and add to the pot of the meat. Scrape the unrefined sugar and add it to the stew. Add some more fat, if needed.
Stir the ajiaco continuously to keep it from sticking or getting smoked. Remove it from heat when ready and opportune to enjoy.

CHICHEME

Ingredients:

1   a liter of purple corn
4   units of unrefined sugar
2   ginger sprouts

Implements:

A cheesecloth strainer, an earthenware pot or jar and a mashing stone

Preparation:

Break the raw purple corn as fine as possible, after washing it right. Then soak it for 20 minutes and refine it again with the mashing stone. Mash the ginger as well. Take a pot of water to heat. Put the paste you made and remain stirring until it boils. Remove it from the heat and let it cool. Then strain it in the cheesecloth; take away the "*payana*" (rubbish). Leave the resultant atol -neither too thin nor too thick- in the earthenware pot or jar.
Add the unrefined sugar broken into pieces and keep it for the next day. Cover it just with a sieve, in order that it can stay aired.

FRIED PORK BRAINS

Ingredients:

1   medium pork head with its offal
5   cloves of garlic
1   big onion
3   spoonfuls of lard
1   spoonful of achiote
1/2 a spoonful of pepper and cumin
2   bell peppers

Implements:

A firewood stove. Thus prepared, the brains get a better taste than by electricity or gas.

Preparation:

Wash the head thoroughly and be careful of taking all the bristles off. Take out the bones, eyes, teeth and parts of the internal ear. Then boil it at high heat, and add the ingredients in the same order they were listed.
Simmer it for three hours. Lower the heat and leave it over the embers.
Remove the head and its offal from the water and cool them down to go ahead mincing them. Put the small pieces in the pot again and simmer it until they get the typical flavor. Calculate the amount of water to use according to the number of helpings.

PORK POZOL

Ingredients:

1   pork head. Besides, the pork offal: tongue, heart, liver,
        kidneys and lungs
5   cloves of garlic, well crushed
1   spoonful of pepper and cumin
1   bin onion
1   big bell pepper
5   leaves of native coriander
        The dice of 2 carrots, 4 potatoes, 1 yucca, 1 chayote, 1
        tiquisque and 1/2 a cabbage
1   minced or sliced green plantain
1   kg of white corn
        Salt to taste

Implements:

Either some ash from a stove or some lime
An empty can for kerosene
An earthen pot
A harvest basket

Preparation:

Put the corn to *nesquezar* (boil with some lime or firewood ashes
until it gets skinned). The operation requires 5 liters of water
with 5 spoonfuls of lime or 500 g of ash, all inside the can.
Once boiled, wash the corn rightly to take the trash away. You'd
better wash it on a basket. Then, wash the pork head as well
(taking its teeth, eyes and ear organs away). Place it in the
earthen pot along with enough water, the spices and the offal.
Boil them.
Softened the head, take it out and mince it quite. Put it to boil.
Then add the vegetables and, when they are softening, add
the minced pork. Simmer everything until it's seasoned to taste.
Please yourself!

BABY CORNCOBS STEW

Ingredients:

500 g of mincemeat
1   bottle of milk
4   ounces of corn paste
2   dozens of baby corncobs (*chilotes*)
1/2   little spoonful of achiote
1/2   a spoonful of pepper
2   small bell peppers
1   sprout of peppermint
1   big onion
4   cloves of garlic
3   spoonfuls of lard
2   spoonfuls of vinegar
3   leaves of oregano
       Salt to taste

Preparation:

In the lard, fry lightly all the ingredients and spices with the meat. Add the baby corncobs sliced. Add two cupfuls of hot water. Put a lid on and let it get boiled.

When everything is soft, add the corn paste dissolved in the milk. It must become watery by adding boiling water. It's a thick kind of stew, never a dry one. Every spice needs have been specially minced.

ZUCCHINI / PIÑUELA STEW

Ingredients:

4 unripe zucchinis or *pipián* (*Cucurbita spp.*; in the first case)
6 flowers of *piñuela* (in the second one)
1 chopped up bell pepper
1 bottle of milk
4 ounces of corn paste
2 spoonfuls of grated dry cheese
Salt and achiote to taste

Implements:

A knife and a saucepan.

Preparation:

Wash the zucchinis and slice them, or chop the piñuela flowers up and wash them thoroughly. Put some fat in a saucepan and fry the spices lightly. Once done, add the slices or the flowers and cover with a lid, to let it get stewed.
Once softened, add the corn paste dissolved in the milk along with the grated cheese. Stir until cook it uniformly. Put the lid again and coddle the stew.

ORGEAT

In Guanacaste, orgeat ("*horchata*") is made of rice and toasted peanuts, thus:

Ingredients:

2 1/2 kg of rice
500 g of toasted peanuts
15   g of cinnamon
2 1/2 kg of sugar
4   bottles of milk
5   bottles of water
250 g of cocoa powder

Implements:

A thin cheesecloth strainer

Preparation:

On the day before, put the rice to soak. On the day to fix it, once drained, grind it together with the peanuts and cinnamon. Strain this paste in the cheesecloth using the instructed amount of water. Dissolve the cocoa powder in the milk and put it to boil. Then, remove it from heat and once it is cool, mix it with the rice. Add the sugar and some ice before serving it.

PEBRE

Ingredients:

1 1/2 kg of corn, lightly toasted and ground like *pinol*, that is
       not too fine nor too rough. Winnow it well in order to take
       the trash away.
1 1/2 kg of meat of iguana or wild boar. As an alternative ribs
       are used.
250   g of lard (some people uses oil instead)
1   big onion
1   spoonful of pepper and cumin
1   little spoonful of achiote
1   finely minced bell pepper
       Salt to taste

Implement:

1 iron pot

Preparation:

Marinate the meat. Put it to boil and add the seasonings. Simmer
it until softened. Take the meat out and keep it aside. Mix the
bouillon with the ground corn and simmer it at low heat. Add
the lard and the salt to the soup. Then go ahead to "*despenicar*"
(chop up) the meat, and put it in the soup again. Stir it
continuously to keep it from sticking or getting smoked.
When everything is already cooked and the corn feels soft,
remove from the heat and serve it. Invite me!

PITARRILLA

Ingredients:

1	a liter of yellow corn
120	g of pepper
120	g of cloves
30	g of cinnamon chips
4	units of unrefined sugar
3	segments of ginger

Implements:

A large earthen jar or pot. A strainer

Preparation:

Toast the corn. Break it dry and coarse and then leave it at rest for two days. The day to prepare it, smash the ingredients (ginger, unrefined sugar, etc.), mix them in with the coarse corn and leave the mix four more days inside the earthen jar. Store or set it in a dry, cool place, to achieve the ferment.

Pour enough water on the jar of pitarrilla and let it ferment. Seal it in and do not touch it again. Then take out the helpings of liquid, add some more water to thin it, strain it and sweeten to taste.

Meanwhile, pour more water on the jar for getting a new fermentation, so that two days later you can serve it again. Repeat the operation of thinning, straining and sweetening.

RESBALADERA

Ingredients:

1   cupful of rice
1/2   a spoonful of vanilla
250   g of sugar
1/2   a cupful of barley grain
1   bottle of milk
     Punched ice to taste

Preparation:

Boil the rice together with the barley until they get cooked. Grind or liquefy it while adding some milk. If you grind it, strain it later and add the remainder of the milk, some vanilla and sugar to taste. Serve it pretty cold and iced.

RICE CAKE

Ingredients:

500	g of husked rice
125	g of softened butter
4	eggs
1	bottle of milk
1	kg of unrefined molasses
2	cinnamon chips
6	cloves
250	g of cheese powder
30	g of achiote
1	pinch of salt

Implements:

Some lightly-toasted plantain leaves
A casserole
An oven
A knife

Preparation:

Wash the rice and put it to soak until the next day. Drain it and boil it. Once softened, add the milk. Simmer it and add the cloves and the cinnamon. Then add the molasses. In no time, add the achiote and the whipped eggs, along with the rendered butter. For thicken the mixture, add the cheese powder. On the casserole, lay a bed of plantain leaves that will prevent the cake from stick there. Pour the mixture on there and bake it until browned. Take it out from the oven and let it cool.
Finally, cut it into slices or squares.

CAJETAS

Ingredients:

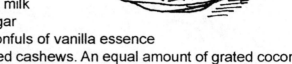

250 g of rice
5 bottles of milk
2 1/2 kg of sugar
2 little spoonfuls of vanilla essence
250 g of broiled cashews. An equal amount of grated coconut
can be used instead of cashews

Implements:

A kitchen counter
A raw corncob

Preparation:

After soaking the rice, grind it pretty fine. Mix the milk with that.
Then add some ground cashews and some entire cashews (if
you are using coconut, add it now). Pour everything on the
casserole and put it at high heat, stirring constantly as needed.
You know it's ready when you take a bit of the mixture and beat
it on a board or on the kitchen counter. Does it harden fast? It's
ready.
Remove it from the heat but remain stirring, until it thickens and
dries up. Then spread the paste on some non-soup dishes.
Give it the shape of circles and decorate them by stamp a
corncob out.

TAÑELAS OR TANELAS

Ingredients:

1   a liter of white corn
3   units of unrefined sugar, or more (to taste)
1   kg of dry cheese
3   eggs
10   cloves
1500 g of fat

Implements:

An oven
A mashing stone
Some lightly toasted plantain leaves.

Preparation:

Put the corn to "*nesquezar*" (boil in some water with some ash) for 15 minutes. Then wash it until taking all the corn trash away. Grind it until making it into corn flour. Aside, grind the cheese and mix it in with the corn flour. Add the scraped unrefined sugar, the eggs, the cloves and the fat. Mash everything with the stone until achieve a pretty fine dough (thin it by a little of water).

 Make the tañelas giving to the dough the shape of small, thin tortillas. Two tortillas make a tañela, thus: put in the center of the tortilla two spoonfuls of a paste of grind cheese and unrefined sugar. Fuse the edges of both tortillas and place them on some greased trays, covered by a bed of plantain leaves. Bake them at a fair heat.

ALFAJORES

Ingredients:

1   kg of white corn
1   unit of unrefined sugar
4   cinnamon chips
1   spoonful of aniseed
1   cupful of water

Implements:

A sharp knife

Preparation:

Toast the corn until browning it. Grind it coarse (not powdered). Blow the corn trash away. In a pot, melt the sugar in the water to make some molasses. Add the aniseed and the cinnamon, and little by little add the ground corn, beating right until it turns into a homogeneous paste. Spread it on a board or table, caring for it gets roundabout a finger in thick. Cool it down and cut it in rhombuses or squares.

BUÑUELOS

Ingredients:

500 g of corn paste
250 g of butter
2   units of unrefined sugar
125 g of grated cheese
125 g of grated raw yucca

Implements:

A basin and a metal sieve or sifter

Preparation:

Put the scraped unrefined sugar into a casserole with a little water to make some molasses. Give it the accurate consistency. Grind the yucca, the corn paste and the cheese together. Add the butter to the new paste and remain kneading. Make some small balls and fry them in bubbling fat. Once browned, shift them to drain in the basin. Already drained, place the paste balls in the sieve and immerse it in the molasses, so that they absorb it.

PERRERREQUES

Ingredients:

50   unripe corncobs
500   g of dry cheese
2   little packs of cloves
         Unrefined sugar to taste
2   eggs
1   cupful of sour cream

Implements:

An oven
Some lightly toasted plantain leaves
A knife

Preparation:

Scrape the corncobs and grind the grains along with the cloves.
Grate the cheese. Scrape the sugar finely. Mix everything. Add
the sour cream to that paste until giving it the desired
consistency.
Take the baking trays and cover their bottoms with the plantain
leaves. Put the paste on the trays and bake it until browned.
Take it out and cut into little squares or rhombuses.
Some people bake the paste for perrerreques over plantain
leaves on small saucepans. Other people wrap the portions of
paste in plantain leaves and make some little tamales, which
are baked too.

PIÑONATES

Ingredients:

2   medium-sized green papayas
2   kg of sugar
     Vanilla essence to taste

Implement:

A kitchen counter

Preparation:

Peel both papayas and wash them thoroughly to remove the sap. Afterwards, chop them finely. Boil the pieces for ten minutes, to soften them quite. Drain them. Make the sugar into molasses and boil it. When it's thickened, add the chopped papayas and stir it continuously, to preserve them. Remain stirring until it gets the desired consistency.
Add the vanilla. By big spoonfuls, take the papaya out and make some little piles of it on a clean board or the counter, which has to be just damp. Let the piñonates dry up and cool.
Then everybody, throw yourself at them!

YOLES

Ingredients:

2 dozens of unripe corncobs
250 g of grated non-fat cheese
125 g of butter
Salt to taste

Implements:

An earthen pot or iron cauldron
A pretty sharp knife
A basin
A mashing stone or grinder

Preparation:

Take the cobs and cut the little trunk off to release the corn husks. Take them out very carefully to keep their natural grooved shape. Place them one by one in the basin. When done, slice the cobs to take the grains out. Scrape the cores of the cob to profit from the corn milk. Grind finely the grains and keep the milk it gives off. To this resultant mash, add the cheese, the butter and the salt.

Lay a bed of the remaining corn husks on the bottom of the pot or cauldron. There boil an enough amount of water. On the other hand, take in twos the husks you kept aside in the basin and set them face to face. Stuff the groove between both husks with four big spoonfuls of the paste you made.

Roll it like wrapping a tamale. Put them in some boiling water for roundabout 45 minutes. Meanwhile, cover this water with even more husks.

The yoles are better cool. Accompany them with some coffee...

MARQUESOTES

Ingredients:

500 g of toasted and ground corn in the shape of fine *pinol*
1 dozen of eggs
500 g of sugar
1 The rind of a green lemon, divided into pieces.

Implements:

An oven
Some fine corn husks
Some lightly toasted plantain leaves
Some *burío* for tying

Preparation:

Whip the eggs and add the pieces of rind. When they are stiff, mix the ground corn in little by little, alternating with the sugar. Set the paste on some greased trays but with a bed of plantain leaves in between so that it doesn't stick. Put the trays into the oven -not too hot- and brown the paste. Then take it out and, once cool, cut it in rhombuses. Wrap them in the fine husks, tie them with burío and give the desired look.

For making the *SOPA BORRACHA* ("Drunken soup"), help each dish to two or three marquesotes, and sprinkle them with some thick syrup blended with a hard drink. Let the marquesotes absorb it, soften and turn doughy.

TRIPE IN SAUCE

Ingredients:

1 1/2 kg of tripe ready-to-cook, diced or chopped
1   pack of elbow macaroni
1   minced big onion
1   branch of celery
2   minced big tomatoes
4   spoonfuls of Worcestershire sauce
125 g of butter
1   little pack of pepper
125 g of grated cheese
     Salt and sugar to taste

Implements:

A boiler, a frying pan and an oven

Preparation:

Boil the tripe properly prepared in some salted water until it softens. Fry the butter and the spices. Add the tomato dice, the Worcestershire, a little bit of salt, the sugar, the pepper and the elbow macaroni –this boiled beforehand.
Pour this composite sauce on the tripe and lay everything on a tray of the oven. When it is rightly browned, sprinkle it with the grated cheese.

COLD (CORN) POZOL

Ingredients:

500 g of a paste made of purple corn
5 liters of boiled and cooled water
Some honey
Vanilla essence to taste

Preparation:

Dissolve the finely ground corn paste in the cool water. Add a touch of vanilla. At the moment of serving, sweeten it with honey and add ice cubes. It's a real delicatessen of the Costa Rican cuisine.

ROPA VIEJA

Ingredients:

All the stale tortillas you have
1 finely minced big onion
5 leaves of native coriander
5 cloves of garlic
1 chopped bell pepper
1 diced big tomato
1/2 bottle of milk
One egg per helping

Preparation:

Tear the tortillas up and soak the pieces in enough water. Season it with the spices and the tomato. Turn that boiler on after adding some fat to it, and when it is just bubbling, add the eggs, taking care of the yolks to not burst. At the full boiling, add the milk and stir all the contents, so that the eggs harden uniformly. The ropavieja is a home, delicious soup.

NICOYA ROSQUILLAS

Ingredients:

1 1/4 kg of white corn
1   kg of pretty salted dry cheese
2   eggs
1 1/2 kg of lard
1   little spoonful of salt

Implements:

A mallet
An oven
A mashing stone

Preparation:

Put some water to boil with enough wooden ashes. On boiling, add the corn and boil it for 15 minutes, stirring continuously until it gets lowered. Cool it down for other 15 minutes. Then, wash it and husk it with the mallet until it releases the trash. Rinse several times until the corn whiten. Then drain it and grind so fine as flour. Grate the cheese and mix it with the corn flour to make a paste. Add the lard, the eggs and the salt. Knead it well, and refine it once again in the mashing stone. There is the secret of this paste: it must be truly fine. Take small portions from the paste one by one, and knead them to shape little bars or sticks. Then close them like rings and squeeze their top edge with your thumb and index, so that they take the shape of little volcanoes. This is the characteristic shape of a Nicoya rosquilla: like a truncated cone.
Set the rosquillas on some thoroughly greased baking trays and go ahead to brown them.
When they're available, you can prepare the following recipe:

ROSQUILLA SOUP

Ingredients:

All the stale rosquillas you have
1   liter of water
1/2 a bottle of milk
     One egg per helping
2   spoonfuls of fat
1   finely minced onion
5   cloves of garlic
4   finely minced leaves of native coriander
1   chopped bell pepper
1   diced tomato
     Salt to taste

Preparation:

Make a stock of the water, fat, spices and salt. When it is just bubbling, add the stale rosquillas. Stir well. Then, break the eggs, being careful of not making the yolks burst, and add them to the stock together with the milk. Simmer it until the eggs are cooked and the rosquillas soften.

TAMAL ASADO

Ingredients:

1   kg of corn (preferable fresh)
500 g of grated cheese
1   kg of sugar
500 g of fat
2   cups of sour milk
500 g of sour cream

Implement:

An oven

Preparation:

Grind the corn so finely. Add the sour milk, the sour cream, the cheese and the sugar while you remain kneading right. Add the fat and stir the paste thoroughly. Put it to boil for a while, remain stirring to prevent it to stick.
Remove it from the heat and shift it to a well greased saucepan. Bake until browning it (to get aware of the extent of cooking, prick it on with a somewhat long stick).
Remove it from the oven and let it cool a little down, to finally cut it into rhombuses or squares.

TAMAL DE ELOTE

Ingredients:

2   cupfuls of pretty unripe corn, scraped from the cobs.
2   spoonfuls of sugar
1   little spoonful of salt
1   little spoonful of baking powder
2   whisked eggs
2   little spoonfuls of paste for tortillas
1   cupful of sour cream

Implements:

An oven and a small earthen pot

Preparation:

At first prepare the corn grating it from its cobs and next grinding it. Do not waste its milk. Gradually add the other ingredients and mix them in. Deal with tasting the degree of sweetness and saltiness.
Pour this paste on the earthen pot and bake it in the previously heated oven.

TAMALES PIZQUES

Ingredients:

1   liter of corn

Implements:

An iron or clay cauldron
Enough vegetal ash
Plantain leaves and *burío* as needed
1 can for kerosene
A wooden bowl
A mashing stone or grinder

Preparation:

In the can, make some thick lye with the vegetal ash and water,
and boil the corn in there. At five hours passed, it is perfectly
cooked. Then wash it to remove the ashes and the trash. Grind
the corn finely.

Take the new corn paste and knead it with some water until get
a smooth paste, such as the paste for tortillas. Once you took
the veins off, toast the plantain leaves lightly. Set two pieces of
leaf as for making a tamale, and put a paste ball of some 90 g
in weight. Slap it lightly just to give it the shape of a tamale.
Wrap each one in the leaves and tie them with the *burío*. Set
them in a cauldron with some boiling water and let them get
cooked. Serve them cool and without any seasoning, but they
own a peculiar flavor.

HUIZCOYOL WINE

Ingredients:

1 kg of huizcoyol grapes
500 g of sugar
5 liters of cool boiled water

Implement:

A glass flask of 1 gallon in capacity

Preparation:

Wash the wild huizcoyol grapes. Crush them softly, or instead cut them into with a knife and put them inside the crystal flask. Add sugar and the purified water. Put a lid on and seal it in, so that it remains in fermentation for one month. At the end of this time, the contents have a flavor like the one of the best table red wines or the finest Vermouth.
It's a popular drink in the flatlands of Guanacaste for the season of the huizcoyol harvest.

TYPICAL MEALS OF LIMÓN

Caribbean

SANDY

RICE AND COCONUT PUDDING

Ingredients:

1   medium coconut
1/2   a cupful of rice
1   cupful of boiling milk
1/2   a cupful of sugar
        Cinnamon powder to taste

Implements:

A thin cloth strainer

Preparation:

Grate well the coconut pulp, and add 3 big spoonfuls of boiling water. Strain it, and squeeze the strainer in order to bring all the coconut milk out.
Wash well the rice, add the coconut milk and put it to boil. When it is just boiling, put the lid on and let it coddle. Once ready, add the boiling milk and the sugar, and remain coddling until it dries up. Place it on a serving dish, and sprinkle with cinnamon powder to taste.

SQUASH IN JAMAICAN CREAM

Ingredients:

1	kg of ripe squash
2	medium onions, finely minced
4	hard-boiled eggs
1	cupful of coconut milk
5	cupfuls of chicken stock (if wished)
60	g of margarine
	Salt and pepper to taste

Implement:

A blender

Preparation:

Peel the squash and boil it in the chicken stock or in 5 cups of water instead. Once softened, liquefy it using the same liquid it was cooked with, and add the coconut milk and the onion, to liquefy them too.
Add salt and pepper to taste, and put it to boil again. On serving, place the slices of egg to float over.

COCONUT CAJETAS

Ingredients:

1   Coconut
1   kg of sugar
1   cup of water
    Some vegetal red

Implement:

A very clean board

Preparation:

Grate the coconut and leave it aside. Put the sugar to cook in the water, stirring constantly, until some syrup is made. Add the coconut, and remain stirring until it is sticky. Without cooling it down, divide the mix into two. Spread one portion over the board, and color the other one with the vegetal red. Place this layer quickly above the former.

CALALU AND CODFISH

Ingredients:

1 kg of calalu
1/4 kg of salted codfish
2 big onions
Some coconut oil

Preparation:

Soak the codfish to remove the excess of salt, and then take the flakes of skin and the bones out. Strip the veins and fibrous parts from the calalu.
Heat the coconut oil. Fry the onion in there, add the calalu, and let it get cooked at a very low heat. When it is pretty softened, add the codfish and remain cooking for some ten minutes more, still at the lowest heat. Serve it hot.

CODFISH CROQUETTES

Ingredients:

500 g of codfish
3 big spoonfuls of flour
1 little spoonful of baking powder
1/2 a cupful of milk
2 branches of parsley
1/2 a bell pepper
1 medium onion
   Chili to taste
4 eggs
   Some achiote
   Some coconut oil
   A pinch of salt

Implements:

A bowl. A frying pan.

Preparation:

The day before, leave the codfish to soak in order that it loses the salt. On the right day, boil it to soften. Discard that water. Scale off, bone and chop the codfish up. Grind it along with the spices. Put it in a bowl and add the eggs besides the flour, the baking powder, the salt and the milk. Thoroughly mixed and kneaded, make some flat patties and put them on a frying pan with heated oil. Mix the oil with achiote to give it some color. Fry them on both sides and serve them hot.

BAMY
(Yucca tortilla)

Ingredients:

2 1/2 kg of yucca
Salt to taste

Preparation:

Peel the washed yucca and grate it. Drain it well and take the tow off. Squeeze it wrapped in a piece of fabric until it hardens. Then grate it again, and put the resultant powder spoonful by spoonful on a frying pan pretty heated beforehand. When brown on a side, turn each bamy round until get a floury, brown tortilla to accompany your meals with.

Keep the starched water you caught on squeezing the yucca. Let it settle, preferably in the sun. Then decant it (pour the liquid off). The remaining sediment is the finest yucca starch.

CHOCLIT TEA

This is the traditional drink at the greatest parties and encounters. It used to be served on Sundays and at the "manteles largos" (celebrating receptions, literally "the smartest tablecloth"). Toast and grind the cocoa almond. Brew it like coffee, blend it with the milk from a coconut and sweeten it to taste.

CODFISH FLITERS

Ingredients:

500 kg of fine codfish
1/2 little spoonful of black pepper
375 g of flour
1/2 little spoonful of achiote
2   eggs
1   onion
1   ripe tomato
1/2 a little spoonful of baking powder
1   little branch of thyme
     Some table oil

Preparation:

Boil the codfish. Drain it and chop it up. Add the eggs, the
black pepper and the onion finely minced, stirring all well. Then
ad the tomato, the thyme and the flour mixed with the baking
powder. If the dough turns out too thick, lighten it with a plus
egg.
Heat a frying pan with enough table oil. Once it is hot, put the
dough spoonful by spoonful in order to get some patties in the
desired size. Turn them over for browning them on both sides.
Serve them hot and accompanied by fried flour patties.

HAMMI-NI

Ingredients:

500 g of white corn
5   cloves
1   pinch of salt
1/2   a coconut grated to take its milk out
1   big can of evaporated milk
        Sugar to taste
500 g of flour dissolved in water
1   cinnamon chip
5   grains of all-spice
1   spoonful of vanilla

Preparation:

Wash the corn up to take the trash away. Boil it with the all-spice and the cinnamon on the prior day. Let them get cooked. The day of the preparation, add to the corn the sugar, coconut milk, vanilla and nutmeg. At once add the evaporated milk, stirring constantly. Simmer everything. Add the dissolved flour. When it's just bubbling, remove it from heat.You can serve it either cold or hot; it's the very same delicacy.

LIGHT CAKE

Ingredients:

750 g of sugar
500 g of margarine
1 kg of raisins
500 g of mixed fruits
1 big can of evaporated milk
1 dozen of eggs (take their embryos away)
750 g of butter
500 g of vegetal fat
500 g of currants
1 bottle of dark rum
2 spoonfuls of baking powder
2 spoonfuls of burnt sugar
1 little spoonful of cinnamon-and-nutmeg powder
30 g of tutti-frutti essence
30 g of pineapple essence
30 g of almond essence (mix the three essences)
2 kg of flour
1/4 of a little spoonful of salt

Implements:

An oven and some molds

Preparation:

Beat the sugar along with the butter until making a paste. Soften it with a bit of evaporated milk. Whisk the eggs without the embryos, and add the paste stirring constantly. Add some vanilla already blended with the three essences. Add the nutmeg and cinnamon powder. Next add the dark rum and the mixed fruits. These mixed fruits as much as the raisins and currants have to have been prepared one or two days before, by immerse them in the dark rum, so that they are soaked in and spongy.

Burn two spoonfuls of sugar in a frying pan until making it blackish. Dissolve it in half a glassful of water. Strain it from the lumps and add it to the paste.

Now, mix the flour, the baking powder and the salt. Once kneaded, unite this paste to the former into the pot and stir them rightly, preferably with a wooden spoon. Prove the consistency by sticking a metal spoon in the paste. Does it stay vertical? It achieved the desired consistency. If not, add a little flour plus to give it body.

Grease and flour several baking bowls and pour the paste on them up to the middle, because it will rise. As an alternative, make a solo cake. Anyway, watch carefully the baking. Prove the baking degree by sinking a sharp knife or a sorghum straw.

PLANTIN THATE

Ingredients:

500 g of fat
1   pinch of salt
4   ripe plantains
30   g of vegetal red mixed with 1 little spoonful of vanilla
2   kg of flour
500 g of sugar
1/2 a cupful of water

Implements:

A rolling pin
A fork
Some molds and an oven.

Preparation:

Boil the peeled plantains and mash then with a fork. Add the sugar and the vanilla mixed with the vegetal red. Aside, mix the flour with the fat and soften it with the water. Once it is some thick dough, knead it with the rolling pin spreading it like dough for cookies. Cut some tortillas with the molds, approximately 15 cm in diameter. In the center of each cookie, put a big spoonful of plantain stuffing. Fold it like an empanada, close its edges and carve them with the fork prongs.
Grease and flour the baking trays and set the plantin thates. Sprinkle them with flour. Bake them, and you'll see them to rise from the tray.

RUNDOWN

Ingredients:

1	kg of fish
2	coconuts
1	yam
1	ñampí
1	green banana
1/2	a medium breadfruit
1	finely minced medium onion
1	minced branch of celery
2	branches of thyme
1/2	a little spoonful of pepper
	Salt to taste

Preparation:

Take the milk out form the coconuts. Peel the yam, the ñampí and the breadfruit, and boil them in the coconut milk. At the full bubbling, when the milk starts to clot and the vegetables are soft, add the previously fried fish along with the spices. Turn the heat into medium and wait for that the milk gets an oily consistency.

Some people prefer boil the vegetables firstly in some salted water, and once softened, move them to the coconut milk, which in their opinion gives to the vegetables a more entire look.

TOTO

Ingredients:

3	kg of flour
1	grated coconut (drained)
2	spoonfuls of cake mixture with almond essence
	Some pineapple essence
15	g of cinnamon powder prepared with nutmeg, cloves and aniseed (everything ground)
4	spoonfuls of treacle or molasses
1/4	of ounce of baking powder
2.5	kg of sugar

Preparation:

Mix all the ingredients (but the flour) in with 6 big glassfuls of water. Once made the dough, flour it quite and put it to bake.

JAMAICAN ENYUCADOS

Ingredients:

1   kg of yucca
325 g of beef
1   ripe big tomato
2   eggs
1   little spoonful of achiote
1   spoonful of Worcestershire sauce
     Salt to taste
     Some fat

Implement:

Some waxed paper.

Preparation:

Grind the beef together with some celery, parsley, bell pepper, onion and chili. Wash, peel and boil the yucca in salted water, but keep it from getting spongy. Drain it and grind still hot. Add the eggs to this yucca paste and knead it altogether.

Put a spoonful of coconut oil on a frying pan and add the achiote besides the ground beef. Remain stirring to keep if from going lumpy. Stew it. Then add the grated tomato and the Worcestershire sauce. Pour just a bit of water now and then, as the beef needs to turn out dry.

On a piece of waxed paper, spread the paste by spoonfuls and compact them like tortillas. Put a spoonful of stew at the center of each tortilla, and join the edges of the waxed paper, to close it. Fry them in enough bubbling fat until browning them. Serve them hot.

BREADFRUIT PATTIES

Ingredients:

1   ripe breadfruit
2   spoonfuls of butter
2   spoonfuls grated cheese
3   spoonfuls of sour cream
     Salt or sugar to taste
     Some frying oil

Preparation:

Peel the breadfruit and boil it for a few minutes. Then puree it
and add the other ingredients, shaping a uniform, lump-free
paste. Heat the oil on a frying pan and put the paste by
spoonfuls, until browning them.
Do you want your patties to be sweet? Add a pinch of cinnamon
and nutmeg.

FRIED BREADFRUIT

Ingredients:

1   unripe breadfruit
     Salt to taste
     Curry to taste
     Some coconut oil

Preparation:

Peel the breadfruit. Cut them in quarters and into pieces of
about half an inch. Sprinkle each piece with the salt and curry.
Heat the coconut oil and brown the pieces on both sides. Move
them to drain the oil and place them over some paper towels,
to take the excess of fat off before serving.

AKI AND CODFISH

The aki is also known in Spanish as *sesos vegetales*. Pick the fruits from the tree JUST when they are quite open. Before, they must not be used, since they are highly poisonous. At the moment of employing them, very carefully take the red vein from every segment, and take the seeds away too. Profit only by the pulp.

Ingredients:

15   fruits of aki, quite ripe and opened by themselves
500 g of codfish
1   big onion
4   cloves of garlic
1   leaf of laurel
3   ripe tomatoes
2   branches of parsley
1   cupful of coconut oil
1   little spoonful of pepper
1   branch of celery
2   cloves

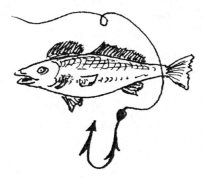

Preparation:

Mince finely all the spices. Soak the codfish for a while, drain it and divide it into pieces. Boil to soften it and discard the water. In the other hand, simmer the spices with coconut oil. Add the codfish, some achiote to taste and the laurel. Add the pepper, the cloves and a spoonful of Worcestershire. Stay simmering. Once ready, add the aki that you have cleaned and boiled lightly for preventing it to shatter. Simmer it until softened. This dish is accompanied with green baby bananas, yucca, ñampí and yam, or also with rice and beans.

IEL
("Agua de sapo")

Ingredients:

1   finely minced chunk of ginger
1/2   a unite of unrefined sugar, quite scraped
10   lemons
      Enough water

Preparation:

Squeeze the lemon juice out and put it to cook together with
the brown sugar and the ginger. Add the water, and let it boil
until everything is well merged. Bottle it in well washed and
boiled containers; seal them with lids. Leave the iel to ferment
for several days.

You can also blend the ingredients and serve it once it is cool,
without waiting for the fermentation. Some people's use is not
cooking the mix but liquefy it still raw; then they drink it. Add
enough ice on serving, since anyway it's a delight.

BROWNED LOBSTER

Ingredients:

1   boil lobster tail
1   chicken stock cube
1   bar of butter or margarine
     Garlic and onion to taste

Implements:

A frying pan and a sharp knife

Preparation:

Render the butter on a frying pan. Add the garlic and stir it. Slice the onion and keep it apart. Cut the lobster shell bellow in half lengthwise. Rub the lobster meat with the stock cube and place it over the butter. Let it brown fairly and move it to a heated dish.

Accompany it with a salad and some patacones. We guarantee there won't be any leftovers...

PAN BON

Ingredients:

8	cupfuls of flour
30	g of baking powder
1/2	unit of unrefined sugar
125	g of fat
30	g of vanilla
1/2	a little spoonful of cinnamon powder
1/4	a little spoonful of nutmeg
125	g of minced crystallized fruits
125	g of raisins

Implements:

A cook brush
An oven and a knife

Preparation:

Dissolve the baking powder in two cupfuls of lukewarm water, along with a third of the flour. Keep it aside for some two or three hours in order that it rises. Melt the unrefined sugar and still on heat add the dough, the remainder of flour, the fat, the vanilla, the cinnamon, the nutmeg and the previously floured fruits and raisins. Knead it fairly until getting homogeneous dough. Divide it into three equal parts and leave apart a little portion for making the "grille". Shape some buns and lay a kind of grille – made of the same dough – on top. With the cook brush, spread some whisked white over the top, to shine the pan bon. Bake them for some 30 minutes. Prove with a knife, an when it comes out clean, the buns are ready. Some people do not lay the little grill, but the simple buns are smashing too.

PATACONES

Ingredients:

2   green plantains
Some frying oil
Salt to taste

Preparation:

Peel both plantains off and scrape them lightly with a knife. Then, cut them into slices of about 1 inch in thick. Fry them lightly. Mash them softly and fry them again, not letting them cool down. Add the salt and serve them to accompany fish and all kinds of seafood.

PATÍ

Ingredients:

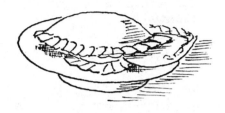

For the dough:
2 y 1/2 cupfuls of flour
125 g of fat
2   spoonfuls of suet
2   spoonfuls of oil

For the stuffing:
1/2   a kilo of mincemeat, or instead finely minced dry meat
1   Panamanian pepper
      Black pepper to taste
3   stale buns or rolls
1   spoonful of minced parsley
2   spoonfuls of finely minced onion
3   finely minced cloves of garlic
3   spoonfuls of oil
      Enough cold water
      Salt and achiote to taste

Implements:

A wooden spoon, a fork, a rolling pin and an oven

Preparation:

Render and mix the fat, suet and oil with the wooden spoon.
Little by little add the sifted flour and the salt. Pour the water on
until shape some homogeneous dough. Knead it fairly and
spread it by the rolling pin. Take care of it to get thin but not
breakable. By using the lip of a glass or the lid of a flask, cut
the dough into circles and stuff them with the meat seasoned
and boiled with the spices. Close them like empanadas and
press their edges with the fork. Spread a little of whisked white
over each patí, and bake them for roundabout 20 minutes. Enjoy
them hot.

ENTIRE FRIED FISH

Ingredients:

1   clean, scaled off, entire fish (ideally snapper, mackerel or kingfish)
3   spoonfuls of coconut oil
    Chili to taste
1/2 a minced onion
1   peeled, minced tomato
1   spoonful of minced celery
    Salt and pepper to taste

Preparation:

Put the oil to heat up in a pan; there fry the fish on both sides. Short later add the other ingredients. Serve it pretty hot and accompanied by a green salad and patacones.

Sandy

BANANA CAKE

Ingredients:

1/4   a cupful and a spoonful of butter
1   cupful of sugar
1   egg
      About 1/2 a cupful of flour
4   ripe bananas
4   tamarinds
1/4   a cupful of cold water
2   oranges
1   little spoonful of nutmeg
2   spoonfuls of thick sour cream
2   crackers

Implements:

An oven and some molds.

Preparation:

Whip all the butter but a spoonful. Add the egg and half a cupful of sugar. Then flour it little by little until getting some hard dough. Knead this, and spread it so that you cover a greased and floured, square mold. Peel the bananas and cut them into pretty thin slices. Set them in the mold and sprinkle them with the remainder of sugar. Soften the tamarinds in the lukewarm water, seed them, mince them and lay over the banana slices.
Add as well the orange juice, the remaining butter, the nutmeg, some salt and the sour cream. Spread it thoroughly and on top powder the crackers.
Bake it at medium heat for some 30 minutes. On serving, cut it into slim slices.

RICE AND BEANS

Ingredients:

1/2	kg of red beans
1	kg of raw rice
1	finely minced medium onion
3	finely minced cloves of garlic
1	leaf of laurel
1	stem of celery
	Salt, thyme and chili to taste
	The milk from 2 coconuts

Implements:

A pressure cooker

Preparation:

In the pressure cooker, boil the read beans along with the coconut milk for about 40 minutes. Once softened, add the spices and the salt. Wash the rice, drain it quite and mix it with the boiling beans. This rice needs to be covered by some 2 inches of liquid, so pour water or coconut milk on it until accomplish that. Stir the mix, put the lid on and coddle it for some 30 minutes, until the rice is ready. Serve it accompanied with chicken or beef in sauce. Mmmmm...

GINGER SAUCE

Ingredients:

4	spoonfuls of vinegar
2	spoonfuls of finely minced onion
1	spoonful of soybean sauce
30	g of fresh grated ginger
60	g of sugar
4	slices of sweet cucumber
2	spoonfuls of cornstarch dissolved in some cold water

Preparation:

Put the first six listed ingredients inside a pot with two cupfuls of water and boil them for five minutes. After, add the cornstarch, stirring to prevent lumps. Cook it for ten minutes. Serve this to bathe meat, either red or white. You won't regret it!

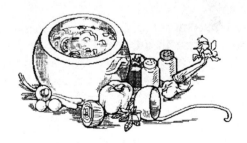

SUSUMBA AND CODFISH

Ingredients:

8 ounces of susumba
8 ounces of fine codfish
2 medium onions
2 medium tomatoes
3 cloves of garlic
2 spoonfuls of vinegar
Black pepper to taste
Some coconut oil

Implements:

A boiler
A frying pan

Preparation:

Boil the susumba for about 30 minutes. Wash the codfish, put it to soak until extracting the salt from it and then chop it up. Heat the oil up on a frying pan and then fry the onion and the garlic (both finely minced). Add the peeled, minced tomatoes and finally add the codfish. Season it with the black pepper. Add the boiled susumba and the vinegar. Coddle it until the codfish is soft.

TACARRY

Ingredients:

4   lobster tails
1/2   a little spoonful of curry
        Salt and pepper to taste
1   Panamanian pepper
3   sliced green bananas
        Some vegetal oil

Implements:

A pretty sharp knife
A frying pan
A fork

Preparation:

Wash the tails thoroughly and slice them without shelling them. Fry them in enough hot oil, stirring frequently. Lower the heat and mix the other ingredients to the lobster. Do not split the Panamanian pepper, but punch it with a fork, and put it entire. Coddle it until the lobster is ready and permeated by the seasonings.

Although this dish owes its name to the lobster and to the curry (*lobsta* + *carry*), you can use crab instead. Try it!

TUM COM MEAL

Ingredients:

4   cupfuls of corn flour
1 1/2 bottles of coconut milk
1   kg of salted pork
     Salt and thyme to taste
2   medium onions finely minced
240 g of dry shrimp
2   cloves of garlic
1   finely minced big bell pepper

Implements:

An iron pot

Preparation:

Firstly, soak the pork to remove the excess of salt. Change the water several times. On the iron pot, pour the coconut milk and add the pork cut into small pieces. Add also the shrimp, the garlic, the onion and the pepper. When the pork is softened, add the thyme, the salt, and slowly the corn flour. Do not stop stirring to keep it from sticking or getting lumpy. Remain cooking for some 20 minutes more, until the coconut milk has been absorbed and the tum com meal is curdled. Shift it to a serving dish and slice it.

YUCCA ROLL

Ingredients:

1	kg of yucca
250	g of mincemeat
1	small bell pepper
1	branch of parsley
500	g of flour
1	small onion
1	branch of celery
1	minced tomato
3	cloves of garlic
	Salt and pepper to taste

Preparation:

Boil the peeled yucca but keep it from get spongy. Grind it and add the flour to convert it into dough. From it, make some little tortillas and put one spoonful of mincemeat over each. This mincemeat needs to have been prepared beforehand thru boiling it along with the spices and the tomato.
Roll every tortilla up like a cylinder and fry them in enough coconut oil until they get brown.

Printed and edited in San José, Costa Rica,
Central America, at

**Ediciones Culturales y Material
Didáctico
A La Tica, S.A.**

sandyescrit@hotmail.com

4a. edition. January, 2005.